Thoughts From the Grief Side of Life

By

Michael Glazier

Dedication

This book is dedicated to the doctors, physician assistants, nurses, and patient care techs. You did all you could to save Kali.

You brought skill, steadiness, and compassion into rooms where fear tried to take over. You watched the numbers, adjusted the plans, explained the hard things, and kept showing up, even when the outcome was uncertain. You carried knowledge, but you also carried humanity, and that mattered more than you may ever know.

Thank you for the late nights, the quick responses, the gentle honesty, and the small acts of kindness that held us together, moment by moment. Thank you for treating Kali as a person, not a diagnosis. Thank you for fighting for her, advocating for her, and caring for her and us with dignity.

In our darkest hours, you gave us hope. You gave us time. You gave us comfort when there was little else to hold onto. Your hands, your hearts, and your commitment will always be part of our story.

With love, gratitude, and deep respect, this book is for you.

Acknowledgment

Kali, I wrote this book for you and in doing so I believe you helped co-author it. Your presence was felt with each word. In helping write it I hope that people will read it and get something out of these poems. If one single person reads these and realizes you can get through grief, even at darkest of times, then the book has been well worth being vulnerable. And they will know their loved one is always there beside them. As for those I have to thank, there are many, and I apologize if I miss anyone.

Obviously, my wife, Allie, for understanding that this is something that at first I objected to, but then it turned into something I needed to do.

My kids, JD, Ashley, Mackenzie, Matt, Rebecca and Anthony, blessed to me by blood and marriage, without them, I might be a wreck, well, more than I am. They are truly stronger than I am.

My Mom and Dad (RIP), I cannot thank you enough for all you have done in my life. I owe you more than I can repay, so I will pay it forward.

My in-laws, Mary, Jeff and Nana as they have been amazing throughout everything in this ordeal, from before the kids even got sick, let alone Kali's passing.

Katrina Etts.... I'm not sure what to say. From the day you gave Kali her ambulance ride to the hospital, the day she was diagnosed with cancer for the second time, you two became friends. Then you willingly became a sounding board for these writings, all while staying busy working on becoming a doctor. You will be an amazing provider, and Kali saw that in you. I cannot thank you with a big enough portion of my heart.

Valerie Mara, who took time from her busy schedule to do a lot of proofreading. Your feedback was heartfelt and has prompted some other poem ideas as well as a reevaluation of my faith, in a good way. I truly appreciate it, probably more than I can explain.

Bob Mara, who deserves more than an honorable mention, you were the link to the care that saved my son's life. Words cannot express the gratitude.

An immense number of other family, friends, coworkers, as well as my employer (who says employers can't be supportive), have been fantastic through all this and more. Your support has never wavered.

A special thanks to the staff at Hartford Hospital CB2---cancer floor---and especially Kali's friend Kristina Lemke. You were her first and last nurse, but a rock during her entire time. I believe she held on one more night to know it was you.

Finally (I think), Janna Phillips LCSW, LMFT, LAC and my grief therapist, who nudged me into doing this. I thought I was tough and could handle this, but without her, I am not sure that I would have. She saw through my reluctancy to be this vulnerable and allowed me the strength to put these thoughts and more on paper. Truly you have been a life saver for me. A thank you, in a book is not enough.

Thank you all, with much love and respect.

About the Author

Michael is an honorably discharged U.S. Marine who has spent much of his life serving others. After his time in the military, he became a volunteer firefighter before building a career as a full-time Paramedic and Operations Supervisor for an ambulance company in the City of Hartford, Connecticut, where he has served his community for nearly 17 years.

Throughout his career, Michael has been present during some of life's most difficult moments for others. While he does not consider himself an expert on grief, his understanding of it comes from deeply personal experience. Over the years, cancer has taken several people he loved dearly, including his sister, his father, and his daughter, as well as other members of his family.

These experiences have shaped Michael's outlook on life and strengthened his appreciation for the time we share with those we love. Through both loss and healing, he continues to move forward with gratitude, guided by the love of his family and the joy found in everyday adventures together.

Table of Contents

Your Shoes and Your Village

It is wise to pick your shoes carefully.

A set of sneakers with a ballroom gown?

Heels with sweatpants and a hoodie?

You would not think to commit these fashion faux pas.

Why, you say—well,

I have run to help others in need,

And I've run from the feelings inside.

I've crawled towards the feet of God

And crawled away when the answer was no.

I have walked down an aisle

with as much joy as I've ever known,

and I've retreated back down it

as scared as I've ever been.

Your closet is filled with shoes for each purpose.

And while you choose your shoes with great care,

so choose the people for your village the same.

For your village is your support—

the ground on which you walk

and that which keeps you grounded.

It's the water at the end of the run,

or energy to start the race.

The blanket that comforts

when the final answer arrives.

They are the anchors of support

in the moment of joy,

And they are the shovels

that dig the hole to bury your fear,

Your shoes and your village—

chosen with care.

Wind Chill of Life

I sit and I ponder

in an EMS crew room, all alone,

wondering what comes next—

the tones of life

Or the "thought of the night,"

as one co-worker called it

(a funny, but reasonably true comment),

seeing as I'm at my computer between calls.

But it is not always about a thought.

Some nights it's about the music,

some the quiet,

some about the breeze blowing through the flags—

flags I'm proud to support

But tonight, it is about all four.

A thought brought on

as I take the trash to the dumpster.

A thought added to

by a favorite cover band,

First to Eleven signing

(amazingly, I may add)

Knocking on Heaven's Door.

The thought is about the breeze—

the breeze causing the wind chill

on this January morning,

a wind chill that rattles us in our bones.

A wind chill we protect ourselves against.

A chill that causes us to bundle up

and warm ourselves

any possible way we can

Grief is no different than the wind chill.

It rattles us.

We bundle up and try to warm ourselves

against the feeling.

We do what we can to protect ourselves.

But as I have found,

you can bundle,

you can hide,

but the chill still gets you.

It seeps through the holes in the fabric,

up the sleeves and down the collar.

And what do we do when it hits us?

We pull it tighter.

We find a warmer place to hide.

But unlike the wind chill,

a warm place doesn't stop the grief—

doesn't stop it grief from seeping in.

The only thing I have found that does

is determination

And even my determination

has its small chinks in the armor,

chinks I never knew existed—

That is, until the word cancer

came from my kid's lips.

Not once.

Not twice.

But three times.

Are you joking?

I got used to sealing the armor,

I did all I could

to keep the heart protected.

But like I said,

grief isn't like the wind chill.

It finds a way in.

then it tears the armor open

like a chainmail shark suit

made of papier-mâché—

More than the weapons I've been trained to use.

Grief uses the biggest weapon of all,

each person with their own.

Mine—love.

Love of a child.

But that weapon isn't just single-barrel

It's got a shot for each kid,

loaded, primed, but unfired,

it's finger never off the trigger.

That weapon, as cold as the winter wind chill,

with a faster fall than the trees unprotected

against the winter wind.

Yet we put the armor back together, hoping—

hoping this time, it will protect,

hoping it will survive the chill.

It won't

But we will.

We have

We do.

What I've Learned

I've learned many a thing in the past two years.

I've learned a picture taken at the right moment can be polarizing

(Me in Marine Corps Dress Blues, kneeling at her open casket).

I've learned people will surprise you—

Both good and bad.

But honestly, more good than bad,

and that gives me hope.

I've learned that when the surprise is bad,

It's truly your response that matters,

Not the surprise.

I've learned I am good at abusing my mind

Past where I thought I could

and still come back functioning.

I've done the same with my body;

It just doesn't respond so easy at this age.

I've learned to have 6 close friends

who you can trust with your life

when the time draws near

are more important than the hundreds

who have passed through

Plus, those six may be carrying you in the end.

But don't forget— those hundreds

did serve their purpose.

Please don't forget the lessons

they taught you.

I've learned I can write

(maybe I did learn something in HS English after all).

I've learned I can make people cry.

I unfortunately haven't learned how to avoid that.

When it comes to crying—

yeah, I've learned I know how to cry,

And I'm really good at it.

I've learned Mom and Dad were right.

I cannot tell you about what

(the list is too long),

but they were right.

I've learned that the toughest

know when to ask for help.

That is a constant lesson

I'm still learning

I've learned that random texts

from friend and family to say hi

are worth their weight in gold.

I've learned I'm good at multitasking.

I can be happy and sad at the same time,

and I can also feel loss and love

congruently.

I've learned that you can get through it.

What *it* is may be different for all of us,

But as long as you keep "walking,"

The storm will almost always stop—

and if it doesn't end,

it slows enough to be tolerable.

I've learned I'm generally a good person.

I've learned that I am not always at my best,

and that is completely acceptable.

I Just can't stop trying.

I've learned that the guidance

of three or four people

has me writing a book,

And I'm ok with this—

even though it makes me vulnerable,

and occasionally I don't feel

I'm good enough to do this.

I've learned that a soft bed

isn't always relaxing.

Sometimes it's the rough sleeps

that teach you how to rest.

I've learned my pain is not judged

one-1 to ten.

It's judged one to twenty-three.

I've learned my kids are amazing.

They are tough, caring, and resilient

and I'm not sure where they got that from.

I've learned that in order to be a good dad,

I first have to figure out fatherhood

(still working on that),

I've learned you should choose your workplace

Not for the money,

but for the support.

I couldn't have gotten through

half of what I've learned

without that support.

Yes, money helps—

but it also hurts.

I've learned it hurts families.

I've learned the age-old adage

in regards to family:

time is the most important thing,

and truly the most undervalued.

What I've learned is this:

I've learned.

I've learned a lot.

I learned I've forgotten

a lot of what I learned—

But I will learn it again.

Tired and Weary

A tired mind and weary eyes—

or is it

a weary mind and tired eyes?

Either way—no matter, no mind.

A combination of both

makes things difficult to find.

It may be asked:

what do you seek

that's out of the view

of my normal mind's eye?

I seek the answers

to questions I have not formed.

I seek support

from the pillars I'm still building.

I seek peace—

Yes, peace, no different than most.

And I seek knowledge,

a knowledge much different

then taught in our schools.

In my quest for these things,

there are things I have noticed.

Sometimes the answer to the question

isn't truly the answer to the question.

After all, do I really know the question?

That pillar of strength

is not what it seems.

It's a work in progress,

built of concrete and steel.

But concrete and steel

are no support for the soul—

Just an analogy at best

for those who show us their strength

at the moments we need to rest.

I seek peace—

something we all desire

with heart and soul and body.

But I've found peace in the search itself,

as it's a constant not to be ignored,

a constant that brings

peace of its own.

But that realization only

Comes from a seeker's perception.

In the search for these things,

with the peace and support

comes part of the knowledge

we so desperately desire.

It's knowledge not of math or science,

not knowledge of language or anatomy.

It is knowledge obtained

from the things we've lost track of:

friendship and caring,

family and love—

the simplest of needs,

filled by those closest to us

and those who have aided in the search.

Truth be told in the answers

they produced more questions.

So we start the search over—

More weary,

more tired.

The Trees

I've planted some trees in your name, Kali,

hoping to bring in new life.

But the life they bring,

the beauty they possess,

fails against the loss of you.

The trees,
though they will be strong and majestic,

Start as a sapling, struggling to live,

struggling to survive another season,

fed by the water and nutrients

contained within the soil.

So do our lives in moments of grief.

We don't vary much from those trees.

Tough bark protecting our insides,

rough on the outside,

not pretty to behold.

Struggling through the seasons,

struggling with what nature

forces into its lives.

Starting its life from the seed,

planted at the moment of loss—

that seed fed by the water,

fed by the nutrients in our lives.

Not food, but love.

The eternal spring we have tapped into.

Our roots searching far and wide.

Once found,

the tree— like our lives—

anchors itself against the seasons,

against the storms,

Hoping beyond hope

the only changes to come

will be that of growth and resilience.

Marked with the occasional changes of color,

the dropping of leaves—

to shed what is old

and prepare for what is new.

Ready to face the next season,

the next storm

stronger than before.

The Should've, Could've, Would've Dilemma

We have all been stuck

in the above dilemmas,

looking back, wondering

if we missed an opportunity.

The easiest answer is yes,

We have all had these thoughts.

It's inevitable when we look

in the rearview mirror of life.

But as the sayings go,

hindsight is 20/20.

It's easy to Monday-morning quarterback.

And while these things are true.

it doesn't change our perspectives

of the "ould've."

I am as guilty as the next,

Possibly even more so.

I should've spent more time with family.

I should've spent less time at work.

I should've let my emotions flow forward

and controlled my anger more.
I should've paid better attention to my education
and should've strived more to show my kids
what was possible.

But we can't dwell on the should've.
After all, there are the could've.

I could've helped more around the house.
I could've helped the homeless man or woman
with a meal.
I could've had one less beer.
I could've thought more about the consequences
and less about the fun in the moment.
I could've said I love you more often.
I could've hated less.

But I digress,
because this isn't complete
without the would've.

If I had known what was going to happen,
I would've done things differently.
I would've have trusted my gut more.
I would've looked at those who dislike me
and realize those opinions don't matter.
I would've wrapped my arms around her

one more time.

I would've realized earlier

that it was bringing her peace.

I would've been the father

they needed and wanted.

In the moments we look back on—

the ones we never expect—

we find these times,

these regrets associated

with the "ould've."

And in that thought process

is the biggest should've,

could've, and would've:

I should've realized.

I could've realized.

I would've realized.

That we aren't above

the miscues of our lives.

We all miss so many moments

to do so much more.

And all I ask in the end

is to learn—

learn the lessons of the "ould've,"

the lessons of the life behind us.

The River of Life

Throughout our lives, we've been taught about different rivers:

the Mighty Mississippi,
splitting the country east to west,

the Amazon,
with all its beauty and danger,

the River Styx,
on which the deceased are ferried.

But little is spoken of the River of Life,

the river on which our lives ride.

The rivers twists and turns,

storms which raise it over the banks,

banks meant to contain its strength,

its beauty, and sometimes

it's fury.

Yet we have many things in common with the river.

Both have shallow waters,

places where everyone can see

what is beneath the surface.

The bends that shape it,

like the tribulations in our lives.

Swift, dangerous waters push us

faster than we want.

The thalweg— it's deepest, most mysterious unknown—

hides things it doesn't want others to see.

It hides what must be protected

and covers it in a murky dungeon,

a dungeon only the brave, or the foolish, dare to search.

For no one knows what lies in wait,

what manner or creature may be found or unleashed,

what type of pain may lie within.

Yet in these moments, we search for answers.

We cross the line into the murky waters,

beneath the comfort of visible light.

We search the depths of our river,

and whether we find what we seek

or it still remains unknown,

it changes you.

it changes your perspective.

And though your river is not navigated by Charon,

the Ferryman of the Styx,

it has transported you

to places you have never known.

It has transported you

to a life changed forever.

The Quiet on Christmas Morning

The packages and cards have all been opened.

The food sitting comfortably in our full bellies.

The laughter of the gathering now distant in our ears.

It's now my time on the couch—

to rest and to recharge,

to reflect on the things that make this time so jolly.

But that is when the trigger of true quiet sets in,

and the memories begin,

brought on by the simplest of things:

the stockings that awaited "Santa's" quick stop,

and so it begins.

You see, the remaining four stockings

still hang in the doorway,

where twelve once were placed.

Two for the daughters a thousand miles away,

one for the daughter that has to work this special day—

those will be sent away in the days that follow.

But then there is one—

the loneliest one,

the one for the daughter who is physically with you no more.

It hangs with no gifts, no cards,

or teeth-decaying candy,

but it hangs in a special place in your mind.

It hangs, filled only with love from your heart.

And in those soulful, quiet moments,

in the depth of your heart,

the stocking brings forth a life—

a life now viewed by the memories burned in your mind,

memories of those Christmases past.

But that single stocking—

green for this year—

is sad but not sad.

And with some of those moments,

you are allowed to be mad.

But alas, it has hung in its place of honor

through the holidays.

Besides the rest of twelve,

all placed with the greatest of care.

To the naked eye,

it appears no different, or special.

But with a Platform 9 ¾ ornament

hanging ceremoniously beside it,

the indication that this one simple green stocking

may be different from the rest.

And to those that know me,

and those that know her,

It's an indication

that this one has a burden to bear.

A burden it throws

on the cold, tired shoulders

of her family—

And friends-well chosen,

in those moments of a true quiet morning.

A burden that it holds

in the strength of its fabric,

busting at it seams

with no object inside it.

A burden much different

than a few years ago,

when its burden was simply

her smile and a thank you.

But this burden it carries—

heavy on this Christmas morning—

does not detract from the beauty it possesses.

And while it's not as elegant as those of the rich,

its function seems quite simple.

but to those who have grieved.

and seen the single last stocking,

Its true purpose to hold more

than I fathomed before.

And on this cold, quiet Christmas morning,

with its burdens pushing at the stocking's fragile stitching,

it holds items more precious

than a queen's royal jewels.

A true, precious commodity:

my memories of twenty-three Christmases past.

The Path

We walk a path to find our life's purpose,

our goals, desires, and dreams hidden along the way,

We navigate the obstacles and ride the highs—
and lows of our successes—

like a real-life Candyland.

We endlessly walk into and out of people's lives,

though not always at our choosing.

We live a path that takes many twists and turns,

and occasionally has an unpaved section or three

We walk the path not knowing

where the end will be,

but knowing what the end will be.

Yet we press on and press forward,

with occasional blinders on,

and sometimes self-protecting tunnel vision.

We seek a goal we know nothing about.

We seek a fulfilment in the purpose on the path.

We affect those who cross our paths,

or is it we crossed theirs?

And along the way,

hopefully giving some guidance

to those who have strayed

from their purpose in life.

However, in our search for our purpose along the path,

maybe we have lost our true purpose.

Maybe our purpose was just

to walk The Path.

The Monster Under the Bed

The noises of your nightime scares,
You struck out and lost the big game.

Screwing up your first real kiss with your teenage crush.

Saying "I love you" for the first time.

Becoming a parent.

Losing a sibling, a parent, or a child—maybe all three

Your own medical issues.

Starting over.

Feeling like you aren't good enough

What does all this have in common?

At each one, you experienced different levels of fear.

At each one, you overcame that fear.

Fear that seemed insurmountable,

beyond anyone else's understanding.

Fear that, while real, helps us stay human,

helps us stay connected.

Fear that made us who we are.

I've been afraid,

even recently been afraid.

Even recently, it seemed insurmountable.

Even today, I will always have a fear.

The fear is why I'm me.

That fear has taught me

to not be truly afraid.

That fear is controlled by one thing—

My desire to beat it.

As I have beaten that fear before,

many times

The Majestic Butterfly

(Or the Animal You See Representing Your Loved One)

People have many animals that represent their loved ones.

For some, a cardinal sitting on a fence.

For some, a blue jay on the arm of a garden bench.

Still, for others, it's their loved one's favorite breed of dog.

For most, different animals represent different loved ones.

For me, one insect happens to represent them all—

the Butterfly

Simple in its beauty.

Fragile,

yet majestic.

How do I know which loved one is near?

It's based solely on timing

and size.

When I need strength,

It's Dad—

larger and more sturdy in their presence.

When I need understanding,

My sister. Sandy—

usually more vibrant and playful.

When I need to be soft and relaxed,

my daughter, Kali—

more fragile wings

flying almost mesmerizing patterns.

Those moments,

when they appear,

bring a different type of guidance—

a kind unspoken,

a kind shared and understood

solely by the intended party,

possibly missed by others.

But how do I know the exact message?

I don't always.

But I know that my life,

in general,

needs that specific message

at that specific moment.

But you say,

"What about when the butterflies aren't around?"

I contest that they always are.

You just need to open your eyes to alternate means—

a different perspective,

a picture from the past,

a reference in a book,

or a TV show.

Our reminders of loved ones will always appear.

And yes, they can hurt

and feel like they come at the wrong time

But they aren't.

It is our view, at the moment,

that is what is wrong.

Did I always believe that

and understand that?

Absolutely not.

And to this day, there are moments

I question—

Until I then realize the message,

the lesson.

Sometimes the lesson is simple:

Just to unload your worries,

even for a little bit.

Like the monarch butterfly migration to me,
it is simply them going off

to offload

the weight we have put on them,

the weight we could no longer bear.

No different then our "backpacks of life"—

a backpack we carry,

not in physical form,

but metaphorically.

A backpack we occasionally need to set down,

and then, unknowingly,

we pick up a lighter load.

Why does it not feel lighter?

Because we are simply tired.

So is the butterfly,

burdened by what it carried for us.

And when the time comes,

when we put the backpack down

for the final time,

we free our butterflies

so they may finally rest.

In the process,

we ourselves become the animal, insect

or nature's beauty

that will carry the burdens

of those who now grieve us—

carrying on the cycle.

This is life.

And death.

The Future

I look to see what the future brings

for me and for my family.

I wonder if it is truly as dark

as it sometimes seems

It makes me ponder what I can do

to change the future.

But in doing so, a thought crosses my mind—

has the future already been changed by my past?

Did what guided my past

already foresee the changes I may make?

Is the future I see

actually the future laid out before me—

the future the past version of me

made changes to become?

Some people believe that no matter the changes they make,

their lives are predetermined,

predetermined in every aspect.

Some believes the Lord controls it all—

that He determines your fate and your future

based solely on your belief.

While others believe we still have a say,

that we can still control our own outcomes.

To know which is the truth is impossible

For every argument for one thought process

can be made for all the others.

Yet I look at the future and wonder:

Is the attempt to change a waste of time?

Is change already controlled by the Lord above?

Have my previous changes already determined my course?

Were those changes all wrong?

Did I choose based on incomplete thinking?

Did I change based on my anger?

Did I change based on what others wanted?

But no matter—

the future is the future.

Your changes,

They can be yours.

They can be the Lord's

They can be predetermined.

It doesn't truly matter who

makes the changes.

Look forward.

Be angry when necessary.

Be sad at times of grief.

Be happy at moments of joy.

Be fulfilled by all the above.

But most of all, be you.

It's the most important thing.

And I've realized—

be changed,

but only when you want to be changed.

The Fight

What's it like to fight the fight

when it's not my fight,

but it is my fight?

It's my fight because the fight isn't just one-on-one

It's one against a village—

a village with strength, love, and hope.

This fight is bare-knuckled and hardcore,

an odds-maker's nightmare.

and not just for him.

This fight—

truly a fight for life.

No cage match.

No rules.

A fight of a body against itself,

where the soul takes the beating

and the heart pumps life throughout the battlefield.

A battlefield where that life, that blood,

is actually the other combatant.

A battle stacked against the home team.

From this battlefield, no one comes out unscathed.

This battlefield can make the weak strong,

the strong weak.

This battlefield creates true resolve.

But in the dewy mist of battle

lies the home team's game changer—

the rock, the pillar, the village.

The village fighting our fight

when we've grown weary.

Fighting our fight

when all seems lost.

The village fixing our soul

because we lost some pieces in battle.

The village changes the battlefield.

The village changes the battle.

The fight's on

Surviving True Loss

Ever wonder what it takes to survive true loss?

Grit and Determination

(with hours of wondering what you did wrong).

Strength of mind

(with equal amounts of wondering what you missed).

Strength of soul

(to overcome the episodes of being a self-punching bag).

A thick mask

(to hide the pain).

Strength of heart

(to handle the answers to questions you didn't want to ask).

Yes.

Yes.

Yes.

And Yes.

But it also takes failure.

It takes depression.

And tears

(lots of tears).

It takes your rock bottom

and lowers it six feet deeper.

It takes words on a stone

way too early.

And then it takes taking one step back—

from the stone,

from the burial,

from the rock bottom.

It takes an openness you may not be comfortable with.

It takes realizing that you thought you were tough before,

but that wasn't actually tough.

It takes a touch,

a smile,

a word.

It takes a moment of light

on a bright, beautiful day.

It takes therapy—

of some kind.

It takes a village

that loved her just as much.

It takes one moment

to realize you'd go through it all again

for the good times.

It takes some courage to accept.

And in that acceptance,
it takes the most simple of things—LOVE

Spoke with God

I spoke with God today.

He tells me you are okay.

He says you light up the clouds.

And I'd be so proud.

But I still can't believe you are gone.

It's broken my heart and soul knowing

that you'll never call home again.

You'll never know the joys of being a parent—

whether kids or dogs—

like the joys I had with you.

That you'll never know the world

that was at your fingertips.

You won't be there

for the amazing moments in your siblings' lives.

You won't be there to lay me

into my final resting place,

to lay a flower at my grave

as a small token of love.

And then I remember

I remember you see it all.

You feel it all,

and we feel your presence.

You guide us when times are tough,

and you bask in our moments.

I realize you will lay me to rest.

You will be there,

welcoming me with loving arms.

You'll make the flowers grow at my grave.

And that you will make one final call home—

ME

Smile, Laugh, Cry

I have smiled

I have laughed

I have cried

But most of all, I have loved

For I have loved my family,

my friends, my life

Do not cry because you miss me

Smile because I made your heart full

Smile because the memories of my life

make you see how special I was to you

And how very special you were to me

Love me, because even in the heavens

I still know your heart

And I feel It

with every beat

Shores

I've been to the shores of a distant mind

And strolled through the beauty

Of what I thought was another's reality,

Pushing off, for a few moments, the harshest of cold truth.

As I strolled forward,

I noticed each of my steps goes in a bidirectional way,

For one takes me further into the pleasures of that place in my mind,

Yet each step in that place

Is a footprint closer to home, in the base of my soul—

A home that my heart has made strong and tough-willed,

All the while being gentle and kind.

A home filled with thoughts of a 100 different emotions,

Thoughts that have churned with the force of a raging river rapid,

Turning over and over,

Breaking against the rocks we call life.

And as we look forward,

We see stillness on the horizon—

A stillness known as peace.

It is not due to the absence of rapids,

But because of our ability to handle the familiar choppy waters,

A familiarity that those who know, know.

A familiarity steeped from a history of pain,

A history dropped on tired shoulders,

Shoulders that bear the burden of hope—

A hope that's filled with countless moments of happiness,

A hope filled with the beauty of a true distant shore.

Roll Into A New Year

There are parts of rolling into a New Year we can't control

(besides control being an illusion),

Midnight will strike.

The ball will drop in Times Square.

People will kiss

(some the wrong person).

The Gregorian Calendar will roll into the next year of our lives.

The news from the day before will not be forgotten.

But to those who have been through significant loss,

there are other parts we can't control.

The grief rolls with you.

It doesn't find a new person to kiss.

It's not forgotten about with the new day's events.

The Times Square Ball doesn't countdown to grief-free.

Midnight struck all around the world

With no change in perspective.

And yet, I still feel like there is new hope.

No—not because the event of grief has moved further away

Or that I have learned to handle it better.

It's that I believe I understand it better.

My grief.

My emotions.

Those who grieve with me

(beside me or in silence).

How do you understand grief?

Well, that is something different for each person,

And how did I begin to understand it?

It's because I started to accept it.

Accept it will always be a part of my life—

a part I can choose to let debilitate me

or make me stronger.

And yes, grief does make you stronger,

Even in its worse times.

Actually, probably the most in the worst times.

Don't ever doubt that.

(I did.)

I did on many levels.

Anything but a funeral.

Anything but more pain.

Anything but further grief.

Anything but holidays without her.

But through it all, we got to another New Year.

But wait—how did that happen?

It happened in a flash.

It happened without me even looking.

But the one-year for her funeral hit.

It hit me hard.

But it wasn't as expected.

It made me realize I survived.

Didn't thrive—

But that's okay.

I survived.

Say it over and over;

Survived.

And if you think about it, it what we do the most—

Even when we aren't grieving.

I survived the Marines.

I survived divorce.

I survived kids

(though that was the best thing to survive).

I survived Paramedic School.

I survive every day at work,

with the possibility of dealing with death.

Maybe not my own—

but death.

And my grief is no different,

No different than what others are about to embark on

through a New Year—

a year of pain, grief and "missing you."

A New Year they are going to roll into at some point,

whether they are ready for it or not.

Does the New Year coming quickly have its advantages?

Yes and no.

As I have grieved through a death early in the year,

middle of the year.

and end of the year,

it has made no difference to my healing.

But I have some unsolicited advice:

Embrace the grief.

In military terms,

"Embrace the suck."

Embrace your family.

Embrace the holidays.

Celebrate the two above.

Celebrate.

The New Years will continue to come.

While the unknown going forward is scary—

especially when you can feel your world collapse—

embrace that scary feeling as well.

Embrace that others—

brothers, sisters, moms, stepdads, grandparents, friends—

are feeling the same.

Roll into the New Year

with a full belly, full mind, and a full heart.

Just roll.

You'll see you survived.

You'll see your strength.

You'll see the New Year.

You'll see.

Trust me.

Perspective and Introspective

P&I

Goes hand in hand

Like grilled cheese and tomato soup

Bacon and eggs

PB&J

Life and death

Wow, that's a lot of thought

And a lot of what has led me to this—

The ability to be introspective,

To give myself a new perspective,

Is something that has taken a lot out of me.

But as the saying goes,

A necessary evil

(like taxes, I guess).

The ability to truly look inside

Is much more then peering through the window.

That window is like stained glass,

Stained by the lessons of life—

Lessons that you don't want to relive,

Lessons that scarred the toughest parts of our souls.

Perspective and Introspective

But what makes us survivors is a special ability—

An ability to wipe the dirt from the glass,

Flip the latch,

Let in the fresh air,

The hot sun,

Let out that which is stagnant,

That which needs a new viewpoint,

And it is at that moment—

That moment of vulnerability—

That Introspective turns to Perspective.

After all,

You learned many a lesson,

Made many a changes

That led to a new way of thinking,

A new way to handle that dusty bottle of feelings.

Crap, it's not really a bottle—

More like a 55-gallon barrel of sludge.

Sludge you have been carting around,

Draining your strength,

Draining your energy,

Weakening your ability to enjoy life's offerings.

It's time.

Time to tap the barrel.

Drop the sludge

(well, maybe not all of it)

Look at it as what it is:

Experience.

Experience coated in crap from life.

Take your new perspectives,

The lessons you have learned,

The pain you've had

since you opened the barrel,

And look at the sludge again.

See if it's still sludge.

Look inside the sludge like it's your own body

(because it is).

Thin it out.

Discard what no longer matters.

Discard the now-unimportant.

Suddenly, the sludge isn't so thick.

Your energy not so drained.

Your strength a little stronger from life.

Your ability to enjoy life

Now slightly simpler.

Because now, when the time comes

To reflect, to be introspective,

Your glass isn't so dirty,

And the air not quite so stale.

And your perspective—

Fresh.

Ready for the next lesson.

Or better yet,

The next adventure.

Pebbles, Stones, Rocks and Boulders

The biggest natural difference—size
But to us, the difference is simple:
Our ability to move them.

Pebbles, stones, and most rocks
Almost always require no help to move.
Yet with boulders, we rely on the help of others.

That is no different than the struggles in our lives.
How we view our struggles determines which version we face,
As well as how we view our strengths and weaknesses
Determines our needs for others.

Facing boulders doesn't mean you can't overcome it by yourself—
It's all the right mindset.
While a pile of pebbles may require the support of your village.

We've far too often got lost in the problems of life.
We've forgotten our strength to move the boulder,
And we've let the pebble trip us in our path.

The approach is the simple key to success.

Moving the boulder or pile of pebbles
Is no different than opening a locked door.
The door—whether the boulder or the pebbles—
Your mindset is the physical key to the solution.

Your determination is the turn of the knob.

The push to open is the "I've got this"

When you tackle your problems.

So face your problems, whatever they may be,

Just like you face the doors in your life.

Use the key,

Turn the handle.

Push.

Then step through the doorway.

Peace and Quiet

Peace and quiet, peace in quiet.
It is their peace, but our quiet—
Our quiet to figure out how to make our peace.

The still of the sound, the calm of the moment.
Their last breath has taken ours,
Time forever changed by a change of forever.

We miss a sound in our ears,
A sound that plays in our hearts,
A sound that pierces the quiet,
A sound that pierces our peace.

We hear quiet, knowing our quiet brings no peace.
We seek peace, knowing it not in the quiet.

But yet, we seek the quiet,
Because we have been taught that it brings peace—
An illusion of the mind, and yet a desire on the soul.

Peace and quiet.
Peace in quiet.

Over It

"Shouldn't you be over it by now"

"Just get over it – it's been long enough."

Stop and think about those statements.

Dually, the most inconsiderate ones I know.

Who are you to decide when I should

"be over it?"

What am I over?

I'm over the fact you don't understand.

It's not your fault.

You've never suffered loss so deep.

I'm over the fact you think you know best.

Only I know what is best for me.

If I grieve till I die,

That is what I will do.

I'm over the tiptoe around me.

Ask.

I will answer anything I can.

I may not be able to explain it perfectly,

But I will try.

I'm over a disease—

A disease so bound on pain,

So bound to take those I love,

So destructive.

I'm over a headstone,

Making sure Kali, my eldest daughter,

Knows Dad is not over loving her,

That he will never be over it,

That he will never truly be over how much it hurts.

But what am I not over?

Your genuine concern.

Your heartfelt wishes.

Your "Are you okay?"

No, I'm not okay.

But I am.

I am because I have to be.

I am because it's what's expected of me.

And I'm kind of over it.

But still, I am okay.

So, what's the next steps to get over…

…………

Unknown.

But a step at a time.

Our Steps to the End

From our waddling first steps

Through the running of childhood,

The calm, calculated footsteps of adulthood,

Back to the frail waddling steps of our golden years,

We've walked what feels like a million miles

And no less then millions of steps.

During those strides of life,

Our feet have kept a steady platform—

Whether barefoot, sandals, sneaker, or heels,

They have done what we have asked of them.

Nature has also paired them with strong support,

Our legs bearing the brunt of the heavy work.

We throw children, backpacks, and occasionally

Other adults on our shoulders, as well as most of our problems,

And expect our legs to stand strong.

They do, with all their might.

Even with all this strength and a steady base,

We occasionally lose sight of the frailness in our steps.

As strong as our legs are,

And as steady as our feet make us,

The simplest of things can cause us to stumble:

Loose rocks that have evaded your glance,

The crack in the sidewalk when running to your favorite jam,

A beautiful sunset,

The sight of your true love when they smile,

The heartache of a loved one gone.

Yes, all simple, but complex.

Rocks loosened by the thousands of steps before yours

(each of those steps with their own story),

The crack of the sidewalk

Caused by the smallest of shifts to the earth,

Sunset—God's gift to end our days

And give us hope for tomorrow,

True love without necessary explanation,

But the loss of a loved one—

The simplest, but probably the most complex.

We all will meet the fate of passing.

It's an inevitable part of life,

For without death, there is no real life.

The complexity arises from the *when,*

The *how,* and occasionally,

The *why,*

The when, I have come to believe, is assigned at birth.

We all have a set time to get in those steps of life.

The *how* may be the unknown,

But it will be shown, sometimes in startling ways.

The *why* is truly the complexity.

It comes when we have run out of our steps,

However predetermined that may be.

Far too often, it feels to early in life:

A father or mother taken before their child is ready,

A brother or sister taken before they may raise their children,

A daughter or son taken before they may make their mark on the world—

Leaving us to question the *why,*

All steps that stopped too soon.

All footprints left in someone else's heart.

When it comes time for those steps to end,

Neither the strength of our legs

Nor the platform of stability of feet have provided

Are a match for the time that our heart and our mind

Have reached their conclusion

MY NURSE

I may not have been your patient,

But you are my nurse.

You are my nurse because I trust my loved one to your caring hands.

You are my nurse because you have words of comfort when I'm speechless.

You are my nurse because you treat me like I'm family.

You are my nurse because you feel the pain my loved one feels.

You are my nurse because you have shed tears by my side.

You are my nurse because the darkness isn't so dark in your presence.

You are my nurse because you give my loved one a fighting chance.

You are my nurse because you are my loved ones' nurse.

Because you are my nurse, you are my family.

Because you are family, you will forever hold a piece of my heart.

—The Glazier Family

7/14/2025

Little Mementos

All through life we spend our time collecting—

Collecting knowledge.

Collecting friends.

Collecting experiences.

Collecting little mementos to remember them all by.

I have a lot of mementos.

Do I remember what each was from?

No.

Do I hold dear those mementos as much as I did at the time?

Probably not.

Probably lost in the craziness of this world,

The craziness of family,

The craziness of life.

The meaning behind the mementos

Has become clouded.

Not because we don't cherish them as much—

We have just learned a different focus,

A different priority.

That priority is different mementos—

The mementos born of blood

(and those adopted or married into).

Those mementos are what really mean something.

Those mementos change over time.

They become new mementos,

But still yours.

Still precious reminders of your life.

Hopefully, a life well spent.

A life well spent on those of family.

A life where the true treasure is not bought,

But still costs a lot.

A life where the treasure is more beautiful,

But more delicate,

More fragile,

And sometimes more easily broken

And harder to fix.

That memento, when it gets shattered,

Creates a ripple.

A ripple that breaks so much more.

It breaks moms, dads, sisters, brothers,

Grandparents, and many more.

It breaks friends.

But mostly, it breaks a spirit—

A spirit inside all of us,

A spirit that was hoping for more.

That memento was more than an object on a shelf.

More than a reminder of days gone past.

But now that memento is not so little.

That memento is a headstone,

Placed six feet above,

six feet above days gone by,

But days not forgotten.

Days spoken of often.

A name never forgotten.

A feeling that surpasses all.

That feeling—

Grief.

In a way, grief is a memento itself.

And not just a memento—

But surviving it is a badge of honor.

A badge earned by a battle,

A battle that never ceases.

A battle till death,

A battle that started with one last breath

And ends only with another one.

The battle rages.

Trust in your strength.

Trust in your beliefs.

Trust in the memories

Stored in your mementos.

The Petals Last Fall

There are many a thing that we see as beautiful:

The morning sunrise on a clear day,

The sunset on a beautiful afternoon,

Moonlight,

Double rainbows after late summer's thunderstorm,

Dew on the petals in the early morning.

What does all this have in common,

Besides beauty?

The ability to relax one's mind,

To get lost in all that nature offers.

I've sat many a time and basked in the beauty,

Drank in the relaxation,

Sipped of a clear mind focus.

It causes me to step back.

To see things in a different light.

It helps me see that all beauty has not disappeared.

It helps me realize

That the petals on roses,

Soon to fall in the cool autumn air,

Are not the only petals that have fallen in my life.

My grandparents.

My sister, Sandy.

My dad, Douglas.

My daughter, Kali.

All parts of the flower:

My grandparents—the pistil.

My sister—the outer petals.

My dad—the roots, the strength.

My daughter—the center petals,

The last one to fall.

And while the petals will all fall,

in 2023,

The last petal didn't fall till a cold December day.

Late in the year, yes,

But it fought.

Fought to hold onto the stem of life.

The petal wasn't ready to give up.

She wasn't ready to drop.

But alas, as it all goes

The time arrived.

The time where the petal drops,

In all its beauty,

Exposing the cold, sharp thorns below.

Thorns that no longer hurt her.

Thorns that shift

And become the punctures

On a family left behind.

Punctures sharp and deep.

Punctures healed not by medicine,

But by time and strength.

And like the last petal lost its strength,

The thorns will slowly lose their sharpness,

Slowly lose their piercing pain,

Slowly become part of nature,

Slowly becoming the nutrients

On which further roses grow,

Helped by those who speak of the roses—

Roses of the past.

Nurtured by those that love them,

By those who care for them,

Those who seek to protect them,

Those who strength has been passed on to them,

Feeding the circle of which we call

Life—Never-Ending.

Last Breath

As you took your last breath with me,

I took my first breath without you.

Or did I take my last breath with you?

I do not know.

For in that moment, I was lost,

But in that same moment, you were found—

Found by the man who promised you no pain,

Promised you would dance among the angels,

Who promised you'd always be by our side.

It was a moment frozen in time,

Yet I feel it wasn't just a moment.

It was the beginning of an eternity—

An eternity of tears and a partial soul,

An eternity of broken dreams,

An eternity of a heart missing beats.

An eternity where you live your dreams,

Where you see the things we can only imagine.

You see beauty and feel calm.

You see the family who we have missed for so long.

That breath was a moment like no other.

That breath changed the heavens.

That breath, that moment, was strong enough to stop a world.

It was our moment, our eternity.

But my world—that stopped.

Kali's Memorium

Good morning.

I'd love to be able to stand up here and say that this isn't hard, that I'm tough enough to do this without losing it, but I'm not going to promise that. There is a song by Tim McGraw with a line that goes, "Who says grown men don't cry?" I know for a fact that is not the truth. Even this uniform doesn't prevent the tears that come from losing a loved one—let alone your child.

Kali was a huge light in anyone's eyes that had a chance to get to know her. Her smile was infectious, and even through her toughest fight, she still managed to smile with all she had at that time. Yes, there were the bad days and the "Daddy, why me?" days, but they were few and far between, given what she was going through.

She had many plans with Christian, who loved her dearly, and their dog Mia—some of which I hope he carries on in her memory. Her siblings, while they did fight at times, each surely each have their own cherished memories—the kind pictures can't fully capture.

Kali did have three of her wishes granted while in the hospital battling. First, she got married to her love, Christian. Second, she got me to walk her down the aisle in uniform. And third, she wished she never would have to learn how to drive— driving was the one thing she was scared she couldn't conquer.

Kali was an amazing young lady and even made the staff at Hartford Hospital CB2 into her second little family. Kristina, Sam, Jess, Stacy, Dr.P (her oncologist) and Dr. Hernon (her surgeon), and many other got to know her and us as if they had grown up together. Their care gave us massive hope, and her strength gave us strength to continue the fight alongside her. I truly believe they left no stone unturned in trying to make her better.

You've all seen the butterfly theme around the room. Butterflies were one of Kali's favorite things, and she often wanted to go to Magic Wings in Massachusetts with her Papa. Now she has gone from our caterpillar to our beautiful butterfly.

While its hard, we know she will never be out of our hearts and minds. She's now with those loved ones who have passed before her. She is in their wings, and we are encased in hers.

Holy Waters of Hell

Yes,

I've dipped my feet where they don't belong.

I've been no angel.

I've seen the things a brain can't forget.

I've caused some pain I can't undo.

I look back through the years,

I see where I have dipped—

Dipped in life,

Dipped in love,

And dipped my feet.

Dipped in the Holy Waters of Hell.

Yes, the Holy Waters of Hell.

Why the Holy Waters?

Because I've done things with good intentions,

Good intentions gone bad,

Gone bad because in hindsight they were

Self-serving,

Self-protecting,

and sometimes careless.

Is this why I now suffer?

Is this why at times I feel cursed?

Cursed to not know what the next call from family will bring,

Cursed to wonder what lies underneath—

Underneath the skin and souls of my loved ones.

A curse,

I feel, comes from dipping my feet where I shouldn't have.

Again, I'm no angel.

But has life prior caused me to know a few?

A few that should not have been so soon,

A couple who toyed with the heavens before,

But had beat the reaper.

So painful.

So not right.

But you can't beat the reaper.

At least, not forever.

A couple that may have paid for the sins from my past.

How can you not contemplate it?

How can you not see the dark water?

A dark water I don't feel can be fully dried.

A dark water disguised,

Disguised to be a saving grace in the moment.

I've dipped my feet in those Holy Waters,

But as I grew, I realized

It was not the Holy Waters.

It was not the saving I thought was coming.

It was a demise.

It was a split to a path that was hard, broken.

It was a path changed by helping—

People helping me,

Me helping people.

But as I sit here, I still wonder.

I wonder if I left part of my soul in those dark waters.

In doing so,

Did that forever link me to the pain from the past?

Does that pain emerge as the pain I've so recently felt

Did they suffer

At the expense of my previous choices?

I understand there is pain no more

For those who have become my angels.

But it is at that moment I believed—

Believed that the "Holy Waters of Hell"

Inflicted its true pain.

A pain it has waited years to inflict

On the one that once danced his way through

Through the most unholy of waters.

Its true pain, now inflicted on my soul.

A pain I will bear in my loved one's honor.

A pain that subsides, even for a moment,

At the sound of their names.

A pain I am happy hold,

For it means I'm still strong.

I'm still surviving.

A pain that means love.

The Holy Waters of Hell

Have not beaten me

Holidays Through The Years

When we were young kids, the holidays were times of joy—

Of family and friends.

During the terrible teens, it became about cash

And as little family time as possible.

(God, I regret that part)

As adults, it becomes about what our significant other is getting us,

What I am getting them, and will it be better.

As parents, it's what are we getting our kids,

What "homemade treat" are they giving to us to warm our hearts.

As a grieving parent, it's about something different—

But still the same.

For the first holidays after,

It's about half smiles and endless tears.

It's about distant hopes and aching fears.

About truly being thankful for everything.

But unable to express it.

It's waiting for the call you know isn't coming,

Because you just left her side—

A side represented by a rock.

It's occasionally an extra beer to fuel the tears.

It's about being muted joyous.

After all, why would I deserve any happiness?

It's a reflection in an ornament,

A reflection that sees inside your soul

And sees the family is still whole.

So what do we do for year two?

We pull on our boots

And warm winter clothes,

And cut down a tree to grace the front of our house.

Play the Christmas carols and sing along.

Hang the stockings.

We fight the tears and find the real smiles.

We continue our hopes,

But know that fears still exist.

We find the expressions for the love that we feel.

We listen above instead of for a ringtone,

As that's where her call comes from.

We still have the extra beer—

We deserve it.

We find the joy in the places we have missed,

Or the new ones before us.

We deserve happy—so find it.

We find that reflection

And continue the brave view inside the soul.

We start to see the family as a whole.

There are truly no pieces missing.

If you truly search the soul.

We hang the stockings with hers right beside.

We still let the hurt rear its ugly head,

As that's when you feel your lost one's love the most.

And when that love really hurts,

You write your thoughts—

Whenever and wherever they cross your mind.

(Even at 2:15 a.m. in an ambulance in front of a PD.)

You seek therapy—knowing it's not a weakness,

But yet a sign of resilience and resolve.

You turn your head to the storm,

Same as the powerful bison that roam the plains,

And you take on year three

Like it's a 5-year-old's Christmas stocking.

Hell to Heaven

From Hell to Heaven

We live life in the middle,

But on the edge of the cliff of desire.

One choice, one action, one thought

Keeping us from the plight of the underworld,

The world filled with Satan's toys—

Toys he dangles in front of life's eyes,

Seeking the souls:

Souls of the weak and powerless,

Souls of the powerful,

Powerful souls with no moral code.

How do we keep from the desires of the devil

When we feel the lord has escaped us?

While I haven't been a religious man,

I know there is the all-protector.

They say his footprints in the sand

Are when he carried us.

But what if it was just a time alone?

A time of reflection,

A time to look forward.

It's also the time I feel the desire—

The desire to give up,

A desire to give in to weakness of grief,

A desire stronger than the joys I've felt.

But the joys seep into the cracks.

The joys fill voids the devil's desire doesn't understand.

The joy builds with each loving memory.

The memories that have brought the grief

Have brought the joy.

Embrace the grief.

Embrace the memories.

Embrace the desires.

But nurture the joy.

For in the joy lies the

One choice, one action, one thought

That keeps the devil's desire

In the devil's playground.

HANDLING GRIEF IS

A LOT LIKE LEARNING

TO WALK

YOU START ON YOUR

KNEES AND EXPECT

TO HIT THEM

OFTEN

GLACIERS

Like the glaciers that cut their path through the solid Alaskan wilderness,

Our lives are cut by the hardships that push themselves into our existence.

Each cut can look beautiful in its own way—

Jagged or smooth,

Forged from a power stronger than itself.

Yet its resilience leads to something shaped to be more beautiful than it was before.

It's outside, forged in ways it never expected.

A core that has hardened with time and stays true to its given values.

The willingness to adjust and be changed shows an understanding for survival.

The force which has changed us has itself been changed by our resistance,

Forever effecting both worlds and both futures.

As that glacier seeks the simplest path through its life,

We, in our existence, seek the same—

Knowing that the places that appear hard, are still the least resistant.

We push and we turn as we change the landscape of our lives,

Leaving in its path, hopefully, an even more solid foundation.

Left with a shell as hard as steel,

But the beauty of untouched nature

Foolish Pride

Have I fooled myself,

Or am I just foolish

To think I'm not angry?

Am I mistaken to think

I've handled this well?

I sit and I write,

To get out the thoughts

Rummaging around in my head.

But as I do,

I wonder—does the soul control,

The emotions instead?

The pangs in my chest when memories subside—

Is that just loss,

or the anger instead?

Like the soul of a monster caged in its place,

Do others see true feelings from the look on my face.

Intermixed with the smiles,

I've had moments of rage,

For good or for bad,

Those times I'm not proud of.

But I've kept the monster controlled,

Knowing full well control is an illusion—

An illusion we've designed to protect the mind.

But the illusion is broken

When we sit and we see

The reality of grief,

The reality we fear,

With our eyes wide open to the feelings inside.

It's when we realize the extent

Of what might have just been—

Our foolish pride,

To think that anger wasn't looming inside,

Using our ribs as the cage

that holds the breath of that monster,

From showing the rage of an anger long held.

I will try, with each breath,

to not feed the monster within,

And hope—with all hope,

And each beat of my heart—

That the foolish pride

Doesn't release the anger inside.

Do you see me

Do you see me?

Do you see the real me?

Or do you see the holes—

The holes I've covered up inside?

The holes created by life,

By loss,

By trauma,

Each hole a different story,

Each hole a change to my life,

Each hole causing a fork in the road,

Forcing me to make a new decision,

A new Path.

Though I'm not always sure it's my decision.

Sometimes the fork is down to one tine—

Then it's no decision at all.

But we have been taught in life

That there are always options,

Always Choices before us.

So what does one do?

You rebuild the other tines,

The other options,

The other pathways,

Yes, it is harder.

Yes, no one knows what happens down that path.

But I'd rather push through the unknown,

Where every step becomes a journey,

Every step becomes a success.

You may climb over a fallen tree or two,

Or in the stretches, reach down for strength

It may be climbing much more then you want

But the toughest climb,

The toughest challenge,

Is that first step.

Know that once you've conquered the step,

The pathway is yours to envision.

Rest on the benches you will create in life.

Take a step back,

Not only to regroup, but to enjoy.

And know the next first step

Will be easier than the last,

And the next step

Will be more important and more rewarding

Then the last—

And the first.

Death Lessons

I have worked many a cardiac arrest,

Presumed a whole bunch more.

Said I'm sorry to a lot of families,

And didn't have a chance to say it to many more.

What I've learned is both a lot and a little.

I've learned death, while final, is not.

Death only stops a beating heart,

But not the spirit, the love, nor the memories.

I've learned that we truly don't talk about death enough.

We avoid the subject like it's contagious.

Society thinks it's a taboo topic.

Blab that shit all day—get it out.

It's not a fire.

Suppression isn't the answer.

I've noticed that the similarities in death

Lie solely in our mind.

Each death is its own beast,

Its own characteristic, its own burden.

I've learned that those who mourn the same death

Mourn entirely different aspects of the loved one,

Of the loss.

I've realized very few are really prepared.

You can say you are ready,

You say you can handle it.

The only preparation is being truthful with yourself.

I've learned that you will remember your loved one

At the most random times,

With the most random memories.

You'll smile the biggest smile

when a clue on Jeopardy brings you a fond thought.

You'll be sad when the situation calls for joy.

It's nothing you can control.

I've learned it can be worse.

What's worse than loss of life of a loved one?

Loss of the memories you cherish.

Forgetting to ever say their name.

Speak their name, for they will hear.

I've learned to accept help,

And to remember

Help isn't always exactly what you were thinking it'd be.

I've learned that, as hard as it is,

Share your story.

The story of your loved one.

Or better yet—the story of your family.

You never know when your words will touch a heart,

Touch a spiritual spark,

Help someone through a dark alley.

Remember: the moment of death, while devastating.

Can be a lesson in life, in love, and in family.

Dark Skies

We see a lot when we look up to the skies.

Each person with their own views,

Each person with a different view of beautiful.

My view is slightly different than most.

What I see in the dark skies—

I see a girl and wonder.

Wonder what she's doing right now.

Wonder how she feels with no pain.

I wonder what was the reason why

She's in those dark skies.

Was heaven hurting

And had a surplus of wings

Is there a battle between the above and below,

Something we don't currently know?

Did they need a soul so strong

To fight off the sinners trying to gain access

To a place they don't belong?

At times, I don't care the reason behind it.

That when I look up, its usually dark skies in my mind.

I do contemplate this, many a time—

Why are they skies so dark

When there is love beyond the heavenly line?

Is it that I don't choose to see,

Through the grief in my eyes?

Or am I mad at a choice they got wrong?

Not that she doesn't deserve the time in the clouds,

But it is far too soon to be allowed.

She'd have had her time in heaven,

Should have been a lot more years—

Plus an additional seven.

Or are the dark skies simply my eyes closed,

Closed to protect me from the pain,

From things I am not meant to see?

I hope not, because I do want to know

The beauty of those waiting there for me,

The beauty of a place not truly known to us,

A place so close but with tickets only one way.

I don't feel like a visit,

And I'm not ready anytime soon

For the call from above

When He decides it to be my day.

As there is unfinished business

With those that I love

Right here

In the beauty of this world,

While being showered from above

With knowledge, guidance,

And a small thing called love.

Dads and Daughters

Every dad.

Every daughter.

Has a story to tell

About love.

And growing up,

And the relationship they've built.

Dads cuddled them with the strongest of arms,

Staggered behind them at the first steps,

Held their hair back as they blew out the candles,

Threatened the boy that first broke her heart,

Held the "oh shit" handle as she learned how to drive.

The thoughts of a father-daughter dance

As he passes on his love.

But the part they don't speak about

Is what they don't expect:

The calm of their lives

Shattered by news,

Shattered by disease,

In one violent breath.

That dropped me to my knees,

Now further bonded by the path before them—

A path built of broken steps,

Broken dreams,

And broken hearts.

I've been there before,

Both with the news of hers and of mine.
Of her brothers and grandfathers alike,

More "Gotta Be Kidding Me" moments

Etched forever in my mind,

With sadness across my face.

And I think, as I process,

I have seen that look before

On a man I know well,

When he had heard the same once before.

But not the news of my daughter—

But yet of his

Cancer again.

She'd had it years prior.

She now walks the broken path

with the man who knows all.

She drew on his love,

His knowledge

And strength

As he's battled the disease laid now as her path.

His oldest of children face down a trampled path,

A path she had walked with strength and resolve.

She draws on the lessons,

Taught through the hardship of truths,

Lessons she passed down to her niece

Through an Angels' quiet words

From the heavens above.

But while her niece has listened,

Her dad has passed his lessons

For her brother to learn.

And like the lessons she passed to her niece,

The lessons from dad came down from above,

Lessons that cemented a connection,

From a dad to his son.

A bond that started a forge a long time ago,

When the first words were spoken

About the cancer with which the family deals.

The cancer we now know

Is not the constellation we see looking up.

It's a disease that's more than

The body and mind.

But back to the connection the cancer did forge,

Of dads and their daughters—

Two generations strong.

But "strong" is a word that grief tries to hide.

Alas, I sit here as the last of four

Taking the breaths of the three from above.

I know with each of those inhalations I take,

Holds another lesson

I am aching to learn.

The Casket

A box.

Simple as it may seem.

As difficult as they come.

Wood, Steel, Soft fabric and feelings—

That is how a casket is put together.

Well, at least in my eyes.

The wood sourced from whatever your heart chooses,

Stained, shellacked and polished to a shine.

Built Strong and sturdy.

Seemingly designed for your loved one,

Bringing about a warmth to a difficult time.

Attached with steel hinges,

Steel decorations adorn,

And steel handles so cold,

Able to carry the most precious of cargo.

The soft fabric,

Your choice for your loved one,

Colors aplenty,

Designed to complement their final outfit,

The clothes they are heaven-bound in.

But what makes a casket a casket?

It's not the wood,

The steel,

Or the fancy fabric.

It's the feelings.

It's the loved one you so dearly cherish.

Without that part,

It's just a box

(no disrespect to casket makers.)

That feeling contained in those confines

Defines a casket.

It is truly what transforms a beautiful design

Into beauty.

And beautiful it is.

Sad, yes, but beautiful.

Worthy of the love you placed inside of it,

Of the memories laid beside your loved one.

Worthy of the trust you place in it

To protect what is so valuable to you.

It's those feelings that make the box

A Casket.

But it also makes it fragile.

Makes it into something you hate.

But it's not the casket you hate,

It's the need for the casket

That causes the hate,

The anger.

But it can be broke,

With strong will

And true focus.

You see past the wood,

Past the steel,

Past the fabric.

You see an amazing sight:

Peace.

Why is it amazing?

Because it is not about us.

It is about our loved one,

Their peace.

Surrounded by trinkets, mementos,

Fabric, steel, and wood,

Family and friends.

Save the anger.

Save the hate.

For I know firsthand,

Leave them at the door.

They have no place

While on your knees
By a casket.

A Million Tears

A million tears have been cried,

Both alone and at her side.

I've tried to wipe away the sadness

From the final goodbye,

Only to cry

A million times more.

I sit now and listen to the silence and wonder:

Is there anything I should have done before?

Did I know before I knew

The pain would be such a dark shade of blue?

I held and I loved,

I prayed for help from above.

At times it felt in vain,

But it wasn't,

As she's no longer in pain.

In her absence I've missed

The warmth on the cheek of a daughter's loving kiss.

In the dark of the night,
it's been so much more

I've felt her pain and her struggle,

which comes with a parents true love.

But I find peace in the fact

That she fought her last fight

Like the nurses beside her,

As no ordinary muggle.

A muggle, you'd say?

And to that, I think not.

Because there was love and magic, deep in that heart.

In fact, I think there was quite a lot.

A Mile

There's a famous quote about judging someone:

Walk a mile in their shoes.

I truly understand the concept.

It goes hand in hand with:

Everyone is fighting a battle you know nothing about.

Some are even fighting battles they don't know about.

I'm not perfect.

I have judged.

I've assumed a person has an easy life.

For that, I am wrong.

I do believe we shouldn't judge,

Especially without knowing

Without walking that mile.

But here in lies my dilemma…

Well, not necessarily my dilemma,

But that of those who judge me:

I DON'T want them to walk a mile in my shoes.

Forget walking in them.

Don't tie them.

Don't slip them on.

Hell, don't even open the closet.

It's not a fun walk.

I personally would rather you judge me.

Yes, it may be harsh towards me.

But it saves you.

You can be wrong about me.

I'm ok with that.

Understand I am fighting a battle.

While it's not necessarily life and death,

(well, maybe it is.)

It is a battle I didn't choose.

And a battle no one should.

But people lose this battle,

And it's not because they are weak.

It's because it is draining—
physically and mentally.

And I admit, while walking my mile,

I have still judged others.

Again, I was wrong.

But what we fail to realize is this:

We don't get to decide for others.

Others get to decide what is their battle.

To me, money—while I'm not rich—

May stress me out, but it is not a battle.

My health—while not perfect—

Not currently a battle.

My battle is grief.

My battle is the health of my family.

And to some people, that isn't a battle.

So, judge me without knowing my battles

I don't mind if you do.

Because to me, judgement is far less painful.

But if you do choose to walk a mile in my shoes,

Understand this (be warned, I guess):

It is not down a pretty forest path

Or a soft beach in the Bahamas.

But on the path lies some enlightenment

Some heartache,

Some adventures,

Some pain,

Some amazing people,

Some disappointment,

Heaps of support,

Occasionally a valley of forgottenness,

And sporadic moments of The Lord.

So be prepared.

Understand the battle—

Someone else's

Or yours.

Hike the boots

(My chosen footwear if you are walking in my footsteps.)

Know you will question often,

About a lot of things—

Questions without answers,

Questions only you can answer,

Questions only answered from your inside.

Enjoy the walk

Or you will miss some of the beauty.

And I am a firm believer:

There is beauty in the pain,

In the walk,

In the hills,

In the valleys,

An odd beauty in the battle itself.

If you understand the battle—

Someone else's

Or yours

10 Minutes A Dad's View

10 minutes to go.

Your senses fear the inevitable.

Your heart rate increases.

A bit of panic sets in.

9 minutes to go

The feeling doesn't subside.

You know there are no changes now.

No chances.

8 minutes to go

Your chest feels tight.

A single breath is an eternity.

Your body starts to fail you.

7 minutes to go

You don't know when it will end.

Only that it will.

How long can this go on?

6 minutes to go

The thoughts are racing.

Overwhelming the mind and body.

Vision starts to tunnel.

5 minutes to go

Is it over yet?

The heart goes faster,

The breathing more intense.

4 minutes to go

A moment of peace?

No—just a moment of clarity.

A moment to understand.

But there is no understanding.

3 minutes to go

Heart rate finally starts to slow.

Breathing still intense but shallow.

Clarity no longer

2 minutes to go

Heart rate feels weak but fast.

Breathing now shallow and inadequate.

It's almost over, but time is irrelevant.

1 minute to go

I'm ready, but not.

Heart rate starts to pound against the chest.

Breathing goes—haywire irregular and burning

30 seconds to go

Everything stabilizes.

Everything peaceful, but painful.

Clarity.

Countdown Over

The last breath.

The last heartbeat.

The last moment before the next.

The last moment in life—changed

This is what my countdown felt like

So, what does it feel like for the dying?

Did she know the end before the end?

Dis she feel the same feeling?

Did she have the countdown?

10 minutes to hell…

And 10 minutes to heaven.

The difference being:

We still have time in hell

Before our time in heaven.

She has made her way through the gauntlet of pain

To the peace of the Pearly Gates,

The Peace the soul has sought.

Whisper on the Wind

I've seen your whisper on the wind.

It spoke of love and happiness,

Of peace and of calm.

Its quiet tone exudes a blissful strength,

Weathering a storm far more powerful than itself.

Knowing the message, it carries

Is so much stronger than the whisper itself.

It must reach its destination,

With the strength of loved ones all about.

But knowing the message may be missed,

It voices what we don't understand.

It prays for the weak to stand,

As it passes on the strength

To those with moments of true weakness,

Born from hurt of missed love.

It does all this

Encased is a fragile thing you loved:

The wings of a beautiful butterfly.

Stories of My Life

The stories of my life

Are saved in the hearts of those who have loved me.

My years in this world have brought tons of love,

and nothing can change the memories.

I had seen this world through eyes wide open,

And now I see down from above.

I know your pain and know your fears,

But know my guidance is forever,

Through the love you have shown to family and friends.

The speckle of me is passed to them all.

Continue the path that you have started,

And know the sound of your beating heart

Is in rhythm with the warm breeze through my flowers,

A breeze that brings back the sweet smell of memories

From times we enjoyed together,

As family forever,

And by each other's side.

Seeing the Devil

I have seen the devil

In a place full of light,

The dawn of a new day

Broken by the angel that has fallen from grace.

With that, we have seen not what is there,

But what the devil has chosen us to see.

He makes us see clearly in the dark,

Yet blinds us in the light of day.

A realm of altered reality,

Designed to push hope below your ability to overcome.

Yet his true weakness lies in his deceit,

As our strength and determination push into truth,

Into the power of the soul—

A strength that the devil knows nothing of.

A soul forgotten in that moment of weakness,

A soul only condemned by the life we choose for it.

In that choice, the devil grins,

For he knows he will lose more then he wins.

But he also knows that around the next corner,

Or down the next block,

Lies a soul not yet claimed by the life of its person.

Those who can see clearly in the dead of the dark

Will chose the light, drawn from the truth of our strengths,

The truths that save a troubled soul from the depths of the darkness,

A soul now filled with strength,

And chosen to be more.

9 798901 902752